SYDNEY · YOUNGSTOWN

40 Rockets

Matthias Media
(St Matthias Press Ltd ACN 067 558 365)
Email: info@matthiasmedia.com.au
Internet: www.matthiasmedia.com.au
Please visit our website for current postal and telephone contact information.

Matthias Media (USA)
Email: sales@matthiasmedia.com
Internet: www.matthiasmedia.com
Please visit our website for current postal and telephone contact information.

ISBN 978 1 922206 15 2

Cover design and typesetting by Lankshear Design.

Contents

Introduction

For more than 25 years I've had the privilege of working with City Bible Forum, encouraging Christians to work together to reach the world with the good news about Jesus through their workplace.

The City Bible Forum team has grown over these years, and now has staff working in all the capital cities of Australia. It's a team that collectively has many years of experience in workplace ministry.

The chapters in this book are all part of the fruit of that experience. What I've tried to do is capture in writing some of the things we encourage Christians in our network to think about and do as they live out their faith at work.

One of the enduring convictions of City Bible Forum is that the workplace is a great place to get to know people and talk to them about Jesus. But as well as the opportunities, our workplaces also present some unique challenges. So we hope and pray that the ideas given here will be useful to many in making the most of these opportunities and avoiding some of the potential pitfalls. Ultimately we hope this book will *motivate* and *equip* you to share the gospel of Jesus Christ with your non-Christian contacts.

The book contains 40 'rockets', each one containing a different idea to encourage you in your evangelism. Why do we call them 'rockets'? Simply because we hope they'll turbocharge your effectiveness in sharing Jesus and get you moving!

The rockets have been written primarily with the workplace in mind, and you'll find quite a lot of references to the office in particular. That's because each rocket was originally written for weekly distribution by City Bible Forum, and our particular focus tends to be on city office workers.

But the advice found here can be applied to other contexts too. Just think about the places you find yourself in regularly, where there are people who don't know Jesus —the school playground, your local shop, the gym... The list goes on, and I'm sure you can think of more. Wherever or whatever your 'office' may be, there are opportunities for evangelism. It might take some extra creativity but many of these rockets can be applied in all sorts of contexts.

How to use this book

Reading this book in one go is likely to be overwhelming, and it might discourage you from putting any of the advice into practice. In order to get the most out of this resource, I recommend you read just one rocket per week, and then work at applying what you've read during that week.

You can read each rocket by yourself or with a friend, or use it as the basis for a small group discussion. Each rocket follows roughly the same format:

- Most rockets begin with a **Stop and consider** point to help you reflect on your Christian life in the workplace at the moment.
- Some rockets are very practical and will give you

an **Action** point to carry out that week. The point of many rockets is to challenge you to start doing something you may not already be doing.

- Because we don't want you just to read a rocket and then forget about it, some rockets end with a **Question** to help you recap on what you've read.
- Sometimes a rocket will be a reminder of who God is and how he is working. The application here (rather than an action point) is to **Pray** and give thanks.
- We've also scattered some review questions throughout the book to remind you of previous rockets and to encourage you to keep applying what you've read in past weeks.

Where it might be helpful for you to jot down some notes, we've left space for you to do so.

If you'd like to find out more about City Bible Forum, visit our website at **www.citybibleforum.org**. You can also receive these rockets as a weekly email by signing up online at **www.citybibleforum.org/rockets**.

Craig Josling

- **“I love the team.”** I enjoy getting to know these people. When I leave and head back to work, I know that I’m not alone. We are in it together—with Jesus.

Action: Are there Christians you know who work nearby who might form an evangelistic prayer team with you? City Bible Forum can give you some tools to get started (see **www.citybibleforum.org/EPT**).[1]

1 If you're in Australia, City Bible Forum may also be able to put you in touch with an evangelistic prayer team.

Use the season to explain the reason

It's amazing that many governments give us public holidays to celebrate and remember the birth, death and resurrection of Jesus. Christianity is on the public agenda at Easter and Christmas (even if distorted). People are in a good mood as they look forward to enjoying the holidays. We should make use of this opportunity to more easily start a conversation about Jesus.

Talking about Easter

Here are some questions you could use to start meaningful conversations around Easter:[2]

- "What is your family doing over Easter? Does Easter have any religious significance for you and your family?"
- "Why do you think Good Friday is called 'good' when it celebrates the death of an innocent man?"
- "Do you think Jesus' death has any significance for us today?" A lot of people will instinctively

2 We'll tackle the Christmas season in Rocket 39.

say "Jesus died for our sins" without having ever thought about what that means. Dig deeper into their understanding, and then explain why Christ took their place.

- "Do you believe that Jesus rose from the dead like the Bible claims?" Again, many people believe this but have never thought about the implications for themselves. Probe their thoughts, and then explain its relevance to us (Jesus is the Lord and Judge, he's coming back, and the Holy Spirit is available to give us new life now—see Acts 2).
- "Have you ever read the account in the Bible of Jesus' death and resurrection?" This might be a good question for people who are anti-Christian but who have never read the source documents. You could offer to give them a printout of Luke 24-26, or a publication that City Bible Forum produces called 'The week that changed the world' (available at **www.citybibleforum.org/theweek**).

Action: What can you do to make use of the season to explain the reason?

Pray: Thank God for your Easter season opportunities. Pray for courage and wise words to start meaningful conversations.

Develop three-dimensional relationships[3]

I went to the funeral of a work colleague's father recently. I met my colleague's mother, sisters, nieces, nephews, and friends from his cycling club. I learned about what sort of man his father was. We grieved together. I knew a bit about my work colleague from chatting around the office, but attending the funeral took our relationship to the next level.

Often relationships can be very shallow and superficial if we only meet a person in one context. Have you ever bumped into an old colleague and struggled to remember their name because they are out of the context from which you know them?

When we only know someone in a work context, we are at best one-dimensional friends. If one of you left the job, the probability of maintaining the relationship would be slim. On the other hand, when you have socialized together outside of work—perhaps even meeting their other friends and family members—then the relationship has every chance of being lifelong. You are also more

3 Rocket 4 was written by Peter Kaldor and adapted by Craig Josling.

likely to get on to more meaningful topics, which can lead to sharing the gospel.

Stop and consider: Think of your colleagues around the office. Do you have a three-dimensional relationship with any of them? How does this affect the way that you relate and the topics of conversation?

Action: What can you do to develop three-dimensional relationships with your work colleagues or clients?

Remember that Jesus is the only way people must be saved

It is easy to feel a lack of courage at work as a Christian. We can feel strong pressure to keep our mouths shut about Jesus. We might fear strong reactions from outspoken atheists, or being rebuked by our bosses, or being viewed as weird.

Stop and consider: What are the forces in your workplace (or mind) that work to keep your mouth shut about Christian things?

'Can' vs 'must'

It can be very motivating to look at the courage and convictions of the early apostles. One of these convictions is that Jesus is the only way that people must be saved. As the apostle Peter says, "there is salvation in no-one else, for there is no other name under heaven given among men by which we must be saved" (Acts 4:12).

The strange thing about this verse is the word 'must' (I'm assuming you already believe that Jesus is the only way).

The apostle Peter could have said that Jesus' name is the only name by which we *can* be saved. This feels better grammatically. But 'can' sounds like an optional extra.

'Must' is stronger and more of an imperative. It seems to imply that there is no choice; we must tell people about this way of salvation and implore them to respond. But why must we, especially in this postmodern world where 'must' is a dirty word?

The apostle Peter's reasons we must be saved

In Acts 4, Peter and John are arrested and brought before the Jewish Council—the same council that sentenced Jesus to die a horrible death just a few weeks previously.

Peter and John have no fear or reticence in speaking plainly about Jesus. They are even trying to persuade the Jewish leaders to turn to him. Why do they believe that everyone must hear about Jesus, even these powerful leaders? You can read their speech in Acts 3:11-26, but here is a summary of their reasons:

1. Jesus has been raised to heaven in awesome power and is coming back to restore God's kingdom (3:21). Healing the crippled man (3:6) was a foretaste of this.
2. If you don't believe in Jesus you will be cut off from this future kingdom (3:23).
3. If you turn to Jesus there is great blessing even now: your sins are wiped out, you will leave your wicked ways behind, and refreshment will come (3:19, 26).
4. Jesus is *the* one predicted in the Old Testament. For the past 2000 years all the prophets have been waiting for him to come and bring in God's kingdom. He is the long awaited saviour. He is the only saviour (3:18, 21-25).

Pray: Ask God to so convict you of these truths that you'd be willing to overcome fear in order to persuade people that they *must* be saved through Jesus.

Be gracious in conversation

The message about Jesus is a word of grace (or God's kindness) to undeserving sinners. This grace should overflow in our words as we speak to people—especially to those who are outsiders to God. As the apostle Paul says:

> Walk in wisdom toward outsiders, making the best use of the time. *Let your speech always be gracious,* seasoned with salt, so that you may know how you ought to answer each person. (Col 4:5-6)

But what should we be doing to make our conversations gracious?[4] Here are some ideas:

- **Make an effort to talk to people.** You might be a shy person who finds it challenging to talk to people you don't know very well. Being gracious will mean pushing yourself to make an effort to be friendly and to meet new people, even when you don't feel like it. Learn to make 'chitchat'. The elevator is a good place to practise this.

4 This verse also tells us that our conversations should be "seasoned with salt". We'll think more about what that means in Rocket 20.

- **Talk about what interests the other person.** People love talking about themselves. Being a good listener and showing genuine interest in what the other person is saying will endear you to them. Even better still is remembering what they said and asking about it the next time you see them. This requires grace, especially when the other person doesn't bother to ask about your interests.
- **Be sincere and compassionate.** It can be easy in some cultures to be flippant and to put others down in a joking way (especially for men). Showing genuine and sincere compassion for people is another way to express grace in your conversation.[5]

So make a special effort to be gracious in your conversations this week. Working on this aspect of your speech might be a precursor to people being more willing to listen to God's gracious word of life in Jesus.

Pray: Thank God for his gracious gospel word to us. Stop now and pray that God will help your conversation at work to be gracious.

Action: Consider writing the word 'gracious' in your diary for the remaining days of the week as a reminder of what you want to be.

5 In Rocket 26 we'll talk about being gracious when responding to conflict.

Keep seeing the wonder of Jesus

Have you ever experienced anything so wonderful that you couldn't help but speak about it?

I remember the excitement and joy of letting people know that I was engaged. I remember the tears of joy as I rang my parents to let them know that our first child had been born. Maybe for you it was the joy of phoning (or Skyping) home to share the experiences of your first overseas trip.

Stop and consider: What wonderful things have you experienced?

Apostolic wonder

For the apostles, the amazing things they experienced in the life, teaching and resurrection of Jesus meant that they couldn't stop telling people about him, even in the face of death threats:

> So [the Jewish religious leaders] called them and charged them not to speak or teach at all in the name of Jesus. But Peter and John answered them, "Whether it is right in the sight of God to listen to you rather than to God, you must judge, for *we cannot but speak of what we have seen and heard*". And when they had further threatened them, they let them go... (Acts 4:18-21)

Often this 'can't help but speak' enthusiasm is found in people who are new Christians. A man from my church named Greg has come to know Jesus recently. While others have struggled to invite non-Christian friends to events explaining Jesus, Greg has invited a dozen. He is so amazed in meeting Jesus that he can't help but speak (and invite).

Keeping the wonder

A challenge for those of us who have known Jesus a long time is to not lose the wonder of it all: the fact that God would come and live among us; the amazing things Jesus did; the spine-tingling truth and challenge of his teaching; the horror of his death; and the awesome power and victory of his resurrection.

So how can we keep the wonder? One idea is to set

aside a few hours on the weekend to find a quiet spot and re-read one of the Gospels of Matthew, Mark, Luke or John in two or three long sessions with a short break in between. Try to imagine yourself there with Jesus, and be amazed again at who Jesus is and why he came.

Action: Schedule a time next weekend to read through a Gospel.

Pray: Ask God to help you see the wonder of Jesus afresh, so that you cannot help speaking about him.

Be open about being a Christian

It's easy to stay quiet about being a Christian at work. We don't want to upset the people we spend 40 hours every week with. We want to be accepted as normal. We don't want our career prospects damaged.

It's easy and convenient to leave our Christian identity at the door after church on Sunday and not bring it into the office on Monday.

Stop and consider: How open are you at work about being a Christian?

Don't give in to fear

It's important for followers of Jesus to be open and honest about belonging to him. There are a number of reasons.

1. Jesus might ignore you if you're ashamed of him

Jesus warns his followers not to be ashamed of him:

> "For whoever is ashamed of me and of my words in this adulterous and sinful generation, of him will the Son of Man also be ashamed when he comes in the glory of his Father with the holy angels." (Mark 8:38)

I don't think Jesus is talking about the occasional lack of courage we all suffer from time to time. After all, the apostle Peter denied Jesus in a big way on the night Jesus was arrested—but he repented and was quickly forgiven. So I think that Jesus is talking here about being ashamed of him in an ongoing and consistent way.

This verse also alerts us to the fact that being open and honest about belonging to Jesus isn't easy. If it were, Jesus wouldn't have to issue such a stern warning to his disciples.

2. Honesty opens the door to conversations

On a more positive note, being open and honest about belonging to Jesus makes the Christian message more accessible to those who don't yet know or believe it.

My friend Mark works for a large insurance company, where he is open and honest about being a Christian. He's also a very likeable guy and helpful when he can be. Mark and his colleague Laurence have worked together for many years, and Laurence has always known that Mark is a keen Christian. So when Laurence was at a point in his life where he wanted to explore spiritual things, he approached Mark for help. This wouldn't have happened if Mark had kept his beliefs to himself.

3. Openness is an incentive to be godly

Finally, if you put it out there that you're a Christian, people will expect you to live up to that. It's not the most noble motivation to be Christlike at work, but it works. You don't want to hear those searing words, "That's not a very Christian thing to do".

Some tips for being more open about being Christian at work

- Put it on your résumé.
- Be upfront about it when you start a new job. When you meet your new work colleagues, and they make an effort to get to know you, this is the time to mention that you're a Christian and that you like to learn from the Bible.
- If you go to an interesting Christian event like a missionary commissioning or a conference, be enthusiastic and mention what was good about it when talking to your colleagues. This helps to break stereotypes of what Christians do with their time; it shows that being a Christian is about more than just going to church on Sundays.
- In conversations where people are discussing an issue that the Bible has an opinion on, say: "Well as a Christian, I believe that..."
- Leave a Christian book on your desk.

NB. Treating people in a Christlike way at work might make people curious, but unless they connect your actions to your faith in Christ, you are just another 'nice person' in the office.

Action: What will you do to be more open about being a Christian at work this week?

Pray: Ask God to help you be unashamed of Jesus in your workplace. Ask him to give you courage and the right words to say.

Ask God to help you endure unjust suffering

Years ago a friend of mine was employed to install a new computerized accounting system for a medium-sized company. He came in after the software had been chosen, and it didn't quite live up to expectations. He did his best, but there were a few glitches as the system came online.

He was working hard and doing what he thought was a good job, when out of the blue he was taken aside and sacked on the spot. Apparently his boss had copped a bit of flak from the board about the difficulties with the new system, so had blamed my friend (behind his back) in order to protect herself. He had received no negative feedback before this. He told me that besides feeling upset and angry he also had fantasies of revenge, which thankfully he never carried out.

Stop and consider: Have you ever experienced injustice at work? How did you react?

God can help

Maybe you didn't get that pay rise you were expecting. "Times are tough", they tell you, "maybe next year". Maybe your boss claimed the credit for your work on a project, or blamed you for their mistake. Maybe you've been overlooked for a promotion that went to a friend of the boss instead. Maybe you feel the injustice of having to keep delivering the same work output with less staff. Maybe your boss takes his or her bad moods out on you with verbal abuse.

How do we respond to all this? How is it possible to keep standing tall and behaving well whilst swallowing the bitter pill of injustice? (Assuming you can't just leave—see footnote 6 below.)

The Bible has much advice and comfort to give when you find yourself in this situation. Here are some helpful things to remember:

1. God commends you for bearing up under the pain of unjust suffering. It's a virtue not to retaliate but to continue to do good in this situation:

> Slaves,[6] in reverent fear of God submit yourselves to your masters, not only to those who are good and considerate, but also to those who are harsh. For it is commendable if someone bears up under the pain of unjust suffering because they are conscious of God. (1 Pet 2:18-19, NIV)

2. Jesus always continued to do good even when he was treated unjustly. Evil men strung the innocent Son of God up on a cross, yet he didn't retaliate:

> For to this you have been called, because Christ also suffered for you, leaving you an example, so that you might follow in his steps. He committed no sin, neither was deceit found in his mouth. When he was reviled, he did not revile in return; when he suffered, he did not threaten, but continued entrusting himself to him who judges justly. (1 Pet 2:21-23)

3. God will bring justice to you one day. Notice in the passage above that Jesus "entrust[ed] himself to him who judges justly" (1 Pet 2:23). Jesus knows that on the day of judgement, God will bring justice.
4. Continuing to do good to those who treat you unjustly will lead to opportunities to share the gospel message (1 Pet 3:14-15; Titus 2:9-10).

6 Are we slaves today in our jobs? The answer is yes and no. Some people are able to leave their jobs and escape injustice by finding a better 'master'. Many, however, are stuck in their jobs and unable to leave because of the fear of not finding another one. They have a mortgage to pay and a family to support. This situation is more like slavery because there is less freedom to opt out.

5. God is powerful and able to change your situation. The apostle Paul recognized how important the prayers of the Corinthians were in him being delivered from danger:

> He has delivered us from such a deadly peril, and he will deliver us again. On him we have set our hope that he will continue to deliver us, as you help us by your prayers. (2 Cor 1:10-11a, NIV)

I know it's not easy, but God can help you bear up under unjust suffering at work, be that now or in the future.[7]

Pray: For other Christians and for yourself, ask God to help you keep trusting in his goodness as you bear up under unjust suffering.

7 There is nothing wrong with seeking justice through legal mechanisms. God has appointed governments to administer justice in this world (Rom 13:3-4). This is especially warranted if it protects other people from getting hurt. However, it should be a last resort.

Don't let work define your value

Stop and consider: Are you feeling good about your work at the moment, or a bit down or unhappy? Why is that?

The ups and downs

I remember a sad old man who used to live in my block of apartments. He used to be the principal of a successful law firm, but lost his practicing certificate because of an anomaly in his trust accounts. He was declared bankrupt and lost everything.

You can be at the top of the pile one day and down the bottom the next. Often it can be through no fault of your own—for example, it may be due to an economic recession or company downsizing.

How will you cope if things go pear-shaped at work? Conversely, will you stay humble and grounded when things go well at work and you're 'kicking goals'?

Grounded in God

One of the great things about being a follower of Jesus Christ is that your self-worth isn't tied up in your work—with all its ups and downs—but is grounded in a far more secure place. You know that you are loved and valuable because God made you and Christ died for you.

See how the apostle James reminds poor Christians of their worth in the gospel, despite their worldly circumstances:

> Listen, my beloved brothers, has not God chosen those who are poor in the world to be rich in faith and heirs of the kingdom, which he has promised to those who love him? (Jas 2:5)

This is incredibly liberating, especially when things aren't going well at work or if you lose your job. Knowing how much God loves and values you can help you to cope even when things are tough.

On the flip side, when things are going really well for you, Jesus can keep you humble and godly (instead of becoming big-headed and proud)—because it's God who gives you the ability to succeed in the first place. As Ecclesiastes reminds us:

> Everyone also to whom God has given wealth and possessions and power to enjoy them, and to accept his lot and rejoice in his toil—this is the gift of God. (Eccl 5:19)

Pray: Thank God that you are valuable because you are his. Pray that you would remember this whether you fail or succeed.

How are you doing with... being gracious in conversation? Have you made an effort to be sincere and compassionate when speaking to people? Have you remembered to talk about what interests the other person?

Leave something interesting on your desk

One of the challenges for Christians at work is to move from the mundane to the meaningful. Leaving an interesting item on your desk or workstation might just be the catalyst to get people talking about the deeper things of life.

You could strategically place a Christian book, or a Bible verse, or an invitation to an upcoming Christian event, or maybe even an interesting newspaper article. Try to think of something that might provoke conversation without being too weird.

Remember that your aim is to lovingly engage people and not to offend them unnecessarily.

Be ready to speak

Always be ready to talk about your interesting item in a way that honours Jesus. People may ask you about it when you least expect it.

In my first office job I wore a fish symbol on the lapel of my suit jacket. Time passed and I completely forgot it was there. One day the general manager of our division jumped in the elevator with me and asked, "What does the fish mean?" I wasn't expecting the question, and mumbled something incoherent. The opportunity was lost. So always be ready.

Keep it fresh

Another tip is to change your item regularly, lest it become part of the scenery of your workstation and no longer stand out. Keep your 'bait' fresh and interesting.

Action: Write on your 'To Do' list: "Find something interesting to place on my desk".

Pray: Ask God to help you find a good conversation starter that's not too weird, and pray that you'd be ready to speak about it when the time comes.

Be sacrificial with your time

One of the reasons I became a Christian was because I lived in a residential college at university and spent lots of time with a Christian guy named Dave. I'm grateful to Dave for sharing his life and faith with me.

In short supply

Time is a precious commodity and in our busy lives it's in short supply. As I've got older, I've found it's been more of a challenge to take the initiative to spend time with my non-Christian contacts. I don't have as much social energy as I used to. After a busy week at work, I'd rather just blob in front of the TV or spend time with friends from church who are easy company. And at work I've just got so much to do.

Stop and consider: Are you pushing yourself to spend time with your non-Christian contacts?

Jesus' example

It's good to remind ourselves that Jesus left the comfort of his heavenly home to spend time with us, in order to bring us back to God:

> Have this mind among yourselves, which is yours in Christ Jesus, who, though he was in the form of God, did not count equality with God a thing to be grasped, but emptied himself, by taking the form of a servant, being born in the likeness of men. And being found in human form, he humbled himself by becoming obedient to the point of death, even death on a cross. (Phil 2:5-8)

Have you ever thought what it must have been like for the perfect Son of God to spend time with us? The Gospel accounts sometimes betray Jesus' frustration with his disciples and with the Jewish people (see Mark 8:17, for example).

The passage above from Philippians says we should have the same mindset as Christ Jesus—we should sacrificially put ourselves out for the benefit of others.

Stop and consider: What do you need to do to spend more time with your non-Christian contacts?

The way forward

Here are some ideas:

- Set aside a day each week where you intentionally try to have coffee or lunch with someone from work.
- Invite a few people over to your place for a dinner party or BBQ. Start early so there's plenty of time to move from superficial chitchat to more meaningful conversation.
- Organize a weekend away with some non-Christian friends.

If you make the effort, it's just a matter of time before the gospel comes up in conversation.

Pray: Ask God to change you so that you would be like the Lord Jesus—willing to put yourself out for the sake of others. Pray for the discipline to plan time with your non-Christian contacts.

Be realistic but optimistic

Your church is organizing an outreach event and is asking for members to be faithful in inviting at least three people along. You agree that the event is worthwhile and are determined to do your bit. You decide to invite three people who you know reasonably well but you've never spoken to them about Jesus. How will it go?

Stop and consider: Are you more of an optimist or pessimist when you contemplate initiating gospel conversations or inviting someone to an event?

What should we expect when we talk to people about Jesus? Are there any grounds for optimism?

Realistic

We have good reasons to expect that many people won't be interested in the Christian message. Jesus teaches that *many* are on the broad road to destruction and *few* are on the narrow road to life (Matt 7:13-14). We shouldn't be surprised or shocked when people respond to the gospel message negatively or with apathy. The Bible expects it, and so should we.

Optimistic

But at the same time we also need to keep in mind that there *are* actually some people on the narrow road to life. The road is not empty.

The Bible teaches that God has chosen some people to respond to his word. God is powerful to change even the most stubborn heart. Therefore, we have grounds for optimism that some people *will* respond positively to the message about Jesus.

Paul's optimism

The apostle Paul knew that gospel ministry would be hard work and that many people would reject him. But he is optimistic that some people will respond positively—because God has elected them to:

> Remember Jesus Christ, risen from the dead, the offspring of David, as preached in my gospel, for which I am suffering, bound with chains as a criminal. But the word of God is not bound! Therefore I endure everything *for the sake of the elect*, that they

> also may obtain the salvation that is in Christ Jesus with eternal glory. (2 Tim 2:8-10)

We don't know who God has chosen for salvation. The only way to find out is to tell the gospel to everyone we come in contact with. Realistically, many won't be interested, but we can be optimistic that some will accept.

There might even be someone sitting in your office right now ready to accept the message of life.

Stop and consider: Do you think you need a dose of realism or optimism when thinking about talking to people about Jesus or inviting someone to an event?

Pray: Thank God that he has chosen some people for salvation. Pray for perseverance to keep proclaiming the gospel.

Get to know your workmates

We all like to be treated as a whole person—we want others to appreciate us in all our complexity.

People at work are more than their jobs. Each person is moulded by their past experiences of family, school, religion, health issues and relationships.

Stop and consider: How well do you know the personal backgrounds of your work colleagues?

Why is this important?

Getting to know your colleagues' backgrounds can be useful in a number of ways. It can help you to:

- **show kindness and compassion:** for example, the young mum who has been up half the night with a crying baby might be moody and cranky in the way she presents at work. But knowing her situation at home will help you to make allowances and respond kindly. And she is filled with joy when you bring her a cup of tea and a muffin. Similarly, the middle-aged man going through a divorce appreciates being cut a bit of slack for his lack of focus at work. His crisis will pass and he'll give back double to the firm for being understood and appreciated when things were hard.

- **build friendships:** knowing a person's background makes it easier to talk to them about the things on their heart. Knowing about their spouse and children, what sporting teams they follow, and so on, will generate a gold mine of conversations and strengthen your friendship.
- **talk about Jesus in a sensitive way:** knowing someone's religious background and other things about their personal life will help you to talk about Christian things in a more sensitive way. I find that asking people (when appropriate) about their family, and if their family has any religious beliefs, gives me a lot of information about how they think about God and the world. This in turn helps me to know the best way to talk to them about Jesus.

  For example, someone who grew up in a family of Jehovah's Witnesses but who rejected that way of life as a young adult might well be suspicious of organized religion. Knowing this background will enable you then to talk about Jesus more personally (and perhaps, at least initially, to avoid inviting them to a Christian meeting). A person with this kind of background is also likely to have a 'saved by works' mindset, so emphasizing our assurance of salvation through Jesus might be the best way to go.

? **Question:** Why is it important to know some personal background information about the people you work with?

Have a sense of urgency

I remember speaking to my elderly aunt who was a Christian. Her long-term friend and live-in housekeeper (Eve) had cancer and her time was running out. I asked my aunt if she had ever spoken to Eve about where she stood with Jesus. My aunt answered, "No, I haven't, but yes, I should try to talk to her about it soon". It was certainly a difficult thing to do, but it was ultimately a *loving* thing to do given that the end was near.

Cynical about Jesus' return

Did you know that the Jehovah's Witnesses have predicted the second coming of Christ at least three times in the 20th century? Each time, many of them sold their possessions, cashed in their insurance policies, and postponed surgery to prepare for Jesus' return.[8]

It's no wonder that people today are cynical about the end of the world and Christ's return. Many people today echo the skeptics of the apostle Peter's day who cried out:

8 JR Stone, *Expecting Armageddon: Essential Readings in Failed Prophecy*, Routledge, New York, 2011, p. 239.

> "Where is the promise of his coming? For ever since the fathers fell asleep, all things are continuing as they were from the beginning of creation." (2 Pet 3:4)

What about you?

Do you believe that Christ will return to earth one day to bring in heaven and hell? I admit that sometimes it's a hard thing to believe. We go to work, come home, go to work, come home, then we rest on the weekend, and on Monday this routine starts all over again. Our lives seem to roll on and on, with no end in sight.

Stop and consider: How often do you think about Christ's second coming?

But the end will come

The apostle Peter answers the skeptics of his day (and the skeptics of today) by saying, "...the day of the Lord will come like a thief" (2 Pet 3:10). Peter is quoting Jesus himself, who warns people to *always* be ready for his coming (see Mark 13:32-37, for example).

If you believe all the other claims Jesus made, including that he was raised from the dead, then is there any reason not to believe that Jesus will also return just as he promised?

And given that we don't know exactly *when* Jesus will return, is it time for you to make more of an effort to share the good news of Jesus with those close to you—friends, family, workmates, neighbours? While you don't want to act like a crazy 'end times' preacher with a sandwich board around your chest, you also don't want to leave it too late:

> Walk in wisdom toward outsiders, making the best use of the time. [The literal translation is "redeem the time".] (Col 4:5)

> So teach us to number our days
> that we may get a heart of wisdom. (Ps 90:12)

Action: Each day this week as you walk into your office, remind yourself that Jesus might come back *today*.

Pray: Ask God to give you more of a sense of urgency to tell your work colleagues about him.

Communicate the cross of Christ

Do you have a mission statement? Lots of people do, often without even realizing it. A personal mission statement might be something like, "I want to be the best person I can be".

The apostle Paul's mission statement was to preach "Jesus Christ and him crucified". Look at how he explains this in his letter to the Corinthians:

> And I, when I came to you, brothers, did not come proclaiming to you the testimony of God with lofty speech or wisdom. For I decided to know nothing among you except Jesus Christ and him crucified. (1 Cor 2:1-2)

Paul's aim was always to preach the message of the cross. To communicate "Jesus Christ and him crucified" should also be *our* aim, because this is still the way God saves people. But firstly, let's be clear on what we mean by the message of the cross.

What is the message of the cross?

Simple

The message of the cross is simple at one level: Jesus died on the cross to save us from our sins, and rose again to be the Lord of all. Remember that the message of the cross also includes Jesus' resurrection (see 1 Corinthians 15:1-7 for Paul's straightforward summary of the gospel).

Complex

But the message of the cross is complex at the same time. Jesus' death achieves justification, redemption, reconciliation, propitiation; it disarms the heavenly powers; and more. And his resurrection means that he is Lord and Judge; that he is coming again; that he is our Great High Priest and the giver of the Holy Spirit. I went to a five-day conference once on the topic of Jesus' death. We studied the Bible from morning till night and still there was more to know. It's a big topic. And if the message of the cross is at the heart of what we should be communicating to people, then we should know it well.

Stop and consider: How well do you understand the message of the cross in all its nuanced complexity?

Action: There are plenty of books that help to explain the message of the cross. How about committing to reading one?[9]

Why does Paul focus on the cross?

The message of the cross is not 'wise' to most people. In fact, the idea that God would kill an innocent Jewish man 2000 years ago to pay for the sins of the whole world is offensive to many people. Add to that the notion that it's *only* by trusting in this crucified man that you will get to heaven, and Christianity becomes even more absurd. On the surface, it sounds like a crazy religion.

So *why* does Paul aim to communicate the cross first and foremost, and not some more attractive, palatable message?

The reasons are threefold:

1. **The cross is God's testimony.** Paul didn't have a choice. He was simply telling people "the testimony of God" (1 Cor 2:1). The cross is God's message.
2. **The cross is a spiritual message.** It's like a car and petrol. The two things are designed to work together. Similarly, the message of the cross is a spiritual message, designed by God to work with the Holy Spirit. The Holy Spirit helps people to understand and then trust in the message (1 Cor 2:12-13). The two work together to bring people to new life.

9 For example, *The Cross of Christ* by John Stott (IVP Books). Or if you want to study what the Bible has to say about the cross, *For Our Sins* by Matthew Jensen is a set of eight studies on the significance of the death of Jesus on the cross (Matthias Media).

3. **The cross humbles.** People who understand and embrace the message of the cross know that they are sinners who can't save themselves. They know that Jesus has saved them by dying in their place. God gets all the glory. You don't have to be brilliant to be saved; you just have to humble yourself (1 Cor 1:26-31).

Implications

Ultimately, if people are going to be saved, they need to hear the message of the cross. I'm not suggesting you never address other topics or questions that non-Christians might have (like Paul does in Acts 17), but ultimately people need to hear the meaning of Jesus' death and resurrection.

Please keep this in mind as you seek to talk to your colleagues at work about Jesus or if you are organizing an evangelistic event.

Keep the main thing the main thing; make Paul's mission statement your mission statement: "For I decided to know nothing among you except Jesus Christ and him crucified" (1 Cor 2:2).

Question: Why does the apostle Paul use the message of a crucified Jewish man as his centerpiece?

How are you doing with... keeping an interesting item on your desk? Have you changed your item this week? Have you been ready to talk about it?

Show joy and love by smiling at people

Stop and consider: How often do you smile? Why? Why not? Where does smiling fit into the Christian life?

Some thoughts:

- **Giving a smile is a precious gift.** I was on a bus recently when a toddler sitting opposite me gave me a big, genuine smile. Maybe you've had a similar experience. Isn't it lovely when a little person (who doesn't even know you) brightens your day with an unprovoked smile?

  Smiling at people is a generous thing to do. It makes them feel good. It says: "I'm pleased to see you" and "I think you're important".

Even Job in the Old Testament recounts happier days before his suffering by saying, "When I smiled at them, they scarcely believed it; the light of my face was precious to them" (Job 29:24, NIV).

- **Smiling builds relationships.** One man working in a broking firm shared some honest thoughts with his work colleague, who had recently resolved to smile more: "When I first came to this office I thought you were a terrible grouch. I have recently changed my mind. You have become more human since you started smiling." Dale Carnegie, an American expert on interpersonal skills, commented on this effect:

  > The effect of a smile is powerful—even when it is unseen. Telephone companies throughout the United States have a program called 'phone power' which is offered to employees who use the telephone for selling their services or products. In this program they suggest that you smile when talking on the phone. Your 'smile' comes through in your voice.[10]

- **Christians are commanded to be joyful and content.** Being joyful and content are Christian virtues. Growing in these should lead to smiling more as you rejoice in God's goodness.

How to be a better smiler

You might be thinking, "Okay, I can see that smiling is a good thing, but I really struggle to make it happen".

10 D Carnegie, *How to Win Friends and Influence People*, Ebury Publishing, London, 2011 (originally published 1936), p. 71.

Here are some tips to help you become a better smiler:

- **Think happy thoughts.** For example: God loves me; God is with me; God has prepared a wonderful future for me in his kingdom; God is in control of the world. Christian truth leads to Christian joy that just might lead to a smile.
- **Look deeply into the other person's eyes** and try to connect with their soul. I know this sounds a bit weird, but it does work. Try it out.
- **Just will yourself to do it.** Start forcing the sides of your mouth up and hopefully the rest will follow. We sometimes do this when posing for a photo.

Obviously this isn't a call to be an irritatingly positive Christian who's never allowed to be sad. But remember that Christian love and joy are often expressed in a smile. Connecting to people in this way might also lead to opportunities to talk about Jesus.

Action: Work at smiling more at people this week, even in the elevator. Try it on the phone.

Memorize Romans 6:23

Stop and consider: Are you able to present the gospel message in a short and compelling way?

Romans 6:23 is a good verse to memorize as a short gospel presentation.

Firstly, 6:23 is an easy reference to recall—you just have to remember that 6 divided by 2 equals 3.

Secondly, the verse works symmetrically in explaining gospel truths:

> For the *wages* of sin is **death**,
> but the *free gift* of God is **eternal life**
> in Christ Jesus our Lord.

You may want to draw it out like this:

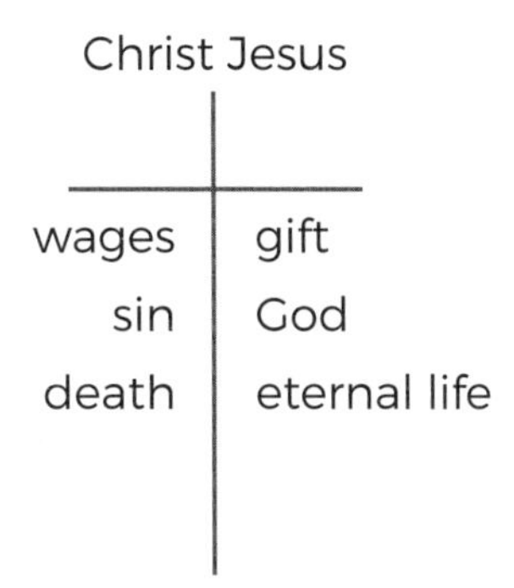

Some things to highlight when explaining this verse

1. A wage is something you earn or deserve, and a gift is something that you are given freely.
2. Sin is not just breaking rules but dishonouring God—it's a relational thing.
3. The wages of sin (what we earn) is death. Explain that in the Bible death is more than physical—it is being separated from God's goodness forever.
4. There is a way to receive eternal life through a gift that God gave us.
5. This gift is Christ Jesus. God sent Jesus into the world to die our death, and to get what *we* deserve. God then raised Jesus to be the Lord of all.
6. We can receive this gift by praying a simple prayer, telling God that we accept his gift and committing to live with Jesus as our Lord. Invite the person to pray a prayer reflecting this.

This verse doesn't say everything we want to say about the gospel, but it says a lot. It's particularly good for people who think it's possible to earn eternal life through works.

Action: Memorize Romans 6:23, practise drawing it out, and then try sharing it with someone.

Challenge others to turn and trust

I dated a girl for six months. We were getting on really well and I wanted to marry her. I was nervous but I finally plucked up the courage to ask the question. Her reply was, "No, not yet".

Was my proposal a failure? In one sense, yes. But it did bring focus to our relationship. We both knew we were facing a serious question: should we spend the rest of our lives together or not?

Putting a proposal to people is a key aspect of sharing the message of Jesus. The gospel message is more than just imparting information; it's also about challenging people to act on it.

Stop and consider: Have you ever asked someone to make a big change in their life?

Turn and trust

In Acts 20, the apostle Paul summarizes his two-year ministry to the people of Ephesus in these words:

> "I have declared to both Jews and Greeks that they must turn to God in repentance and have faith [trust] in our Lord Jesus." (Acts 20:21, NIV)

Here are four things to note about Paul's call to turn and trust:

1. **It's universal.** The call is to *everyone* he preaches to, both Jews and Gentiles. There are no exceptions.
2. **It's not an optional extra.** Paul *declares* that people *must* do it. These are strong imperatives challenging people to respond. This is challenging for us in our postmodern age, where you're not supposed to tell people (especially in such strong language) that they need to change.
3. **It's a call to action.** We are to turn *to* God. By urging people to turn to God, Paul assumes that a person's default position is to have their back to God—they're turned *away* from God; they're ignoring him. This call to turn *to* God also assumes that they have had their eyes and heart focused on other things. So the challenge now is to make God the number one priority in their life.
4. **It's a call to have faith.** We are to trust *in Jesus*. We need to trust that:
   a. Jesus is the risen Lord and Judge of the world (Acts 17:30-31)
   b. Jesus is our Saviour, who has paid for our sins when he died on the cross (Rom 3:21-28).

Eventually...

I've read the Bible with many people enquiring into Christianity. We cover all the key bits of information about the Christian faith, but eventually I have to ask them: "What do you think? What are you going to do about the claims of Jesus?"[11] I have to invite them to turn to God and trust Jesus.

Nothing ventured, nothing gained

I dread having to ask this question because I fear they will say "No", and all my efforts might have been wasted. But part of sharing the Christian gospel is the call to repentance and faith. And guess what? Some people are glad to respond and say yes... just like my wife eventually did when I again asked her to marry me, a few months after the first proposal!

Action: Is there someone you need to invite to turn to God and trust in Jesus? Maybe it's someone you've been reading the Bible with. Or maybe there's someone at church who you suspect might never have done this. Plan when and how you might gently and lovingly encourage them to turn to God, and pray about it.

11 Sometimes it's okay for a person to hear the call to turn and trust even before they have all the information about what they are turning to and what they are trusting in. This communicates that Christianity demands a total change of life and that it's a serious commitment—so they know they'd better check it out thoroughly.

Move conversations from the mundane to the meaningful

Recipe for godly conversations

1 x measure of graciousness
1 x measure of saltiness
Stir thoroughly, adding prayer and courage

In Rocket 6 we looked at Colossians 4:6, which encourages us to be gracious in our speech. This same verse also encourages us to season our conversations with salt:

> Let your speech always be gracious, *seasoned with salt*, so that you may know how you ought to answer each person. (Col 4:6)

What does 'seasoned with salt' mean?

Salt provides seasoning or flavour (see also Job 6:6). So a 'salty' conversation is one that is not bland or dull but has a bit of spice in it. It's provocative conversation that will challenge people to move beyond the mundane to the meaningful.

An example

A man recently shared with me a stressful situation he is in with a dodgy, deceitful and money-hungry builder. I listened carefully and empathized with him. I was gracious. But I could have been more 'salty' by saying, "Why are people like that?" or "I can tell this is a worry for you. I'm a Christian—would you mind if I prayed for you?" I think he would have appreciated it.

Stop and consider: Do you think you need to add more graciousness to your conversations with unbelievers, or do you need to add more salt?

A challenge

Being 'salty' in our conversations is a challenge to some of us. It takes courage to take a risk and say something provocative. Maybe these suggestions will help you to be more 'salty'.

- As per my example above, **offer to pray** for people who are anxious.
- Try to **move conversations to deeper topics**—things like the purpose of life, human nature, or life after death. For example, some news reports referred to the shooting down of Malaysian Airlines flight MH17 as an "evil" act. You could ask, "What makes

that an evil act?" or "Why do people do stuff like that?" And see where the conversation leads.

- If people are talking more deeply about an issue, throw in, "As a Christian I believe..." and **give a biblical perspective on the issue**.
- Recognize and **articulate God's sovereignty** over all of life. For example, you could say, "I'll see you tomorrow, God willing" or "Thank God for the rain yesterday; my garden was so dry".

Remember, our aim in every conversation is to try to turn the discussion (in a natural way) to the most interesting person of all: Jesus Christ. He is the ultimate 'salt', who gives flavour and richness to life.

? **Question:** What does it mean to have 'salty' conversations? What are some examples of this?

Action: This week make an effort to have more 'salty' conversations with your non-Christian work colleagues. See where this leads.

How are you doing with... memorizing Romans 6:23? Have you tried to explain it to somebody?

Remember you're in a spiritual battle

We live in a material world—a world we can touch and see and smell and taste. But the Bible reminds us that there is an unseen *spiritual* battle going on around us that we need to be very aware of:

> For we do not wrestle against flesh and blood, but against the rulers, against the authorities, against the cosmic powers over this present darkness, against the spiritual forces of evil in the heavenly places. (Eph 6:12)

Stop and consider: How conscious are you of the spiritual battle going on around you?

The devil's work

> ...the god of this world has blinded the minds of the unbelievers, to keep them from seeing the light of the gospel of the glory of Christ, who is the image of God. (2 Cor 4:4)

This verse reminds us that the devil is at work deceiving people. He is putting false thoughts in their minds so that they will not turn to Christ. Thoughts like: "God doesn't exist" or "The Christian message is outdated" or "I'm better off trying to live without God" or "Don't think about the future—everything will be okay" or "Just live for the moment".

The devil is also trying to destroy the confidence of Christians, by telling them things like: "You're too busy to read God's word" or "Prayer doesn't do anything" or "You can follow Christ and have the world as well" or "Just relax and take it easy" or "Don't upset people with that embarrassing gospel message".

Take your stand against the devil's schemes

The devil does his best work when we forget he is there. But when I remember that there is a spiritual battle raging around me, I'm driven to pray with more fervour; to be more alert as I read the Bible; to be more confident that the message of the cross comes with the power of the Holy Spirit to save and change people.

> ...be strong in the Lord and in the strength of his might. Put on the whole armour of God, that you may be able to stand against the schemes of the devil. (Eph 6:10-11)

Action: This week pause for a minute each day to remember the spiritual battle going on around you, and pray for the souls of the people in your workplace.

Put on an outreach event at work

Carol felt the cool rush of the air conditioning as she entered the Telstra building as usual on Monday morning.

As she caught the elevator to the 22nd floor she noticed a small poster on the panel next to her. It was an invitation to a talk on connecting with God, to be held on level 5 that day. The fact that a free lunch was included sealed the deal. "Why not?", she thought as she made up her mind to go along. Carol heard the gospel clearly that day at Telstra. She asked questions after the talk and was keen to read a book on the historicity of Christianity.

Five benefits of an outreach event at work

There are at least five benefits in putting on an outreach event at your workplace:

1. It's in a familiar environment for guests; it's on their turf.
2. Invited guests are more likely to know others.
3. It's time-efficient (i.e. one hour at lunchtime).
4. It's easy to get to—people will only need to walk down the corridor or catch the elevator.
5. Follow-up events are similarly convenient to attend.

Compare this to trying to invite a work colleague to a church-based outreach event. Your church might be a long way from where they live, so attending the event might require hours of their time, plus you're asking them to come onto unfamiliar turf.

What to put on

The options for workplace outreach events are many and varied. Here are three examples of what I've found has worked well:

1. **A large, talk-based event:** Form a committee of like-minded Christians. Find a good outside speaker with a catchy topic. Book a room and organize food. Pray, advertise, invite, follow-up. The week before Easter is a good time to put something on.
2. **A multimedia event:** Invite friends from work to watch *The Christ Files* documentary on the historicity of Christianity. It's a really well-produced presentation with four 26-minute sessions.[12] Finish each session with a time for discussion.
3. **A boutique event:** Invite a few friends to lunch to share with them what you enjoy about being a Christian. Start by explaining briefly what a Christian is.

It's really worth it

Putting on an outreach event at work requires courage and a little planning, but experience has shown this is one of the most effective ways of getting people to consider the Christian message.

12 For more information, visit www.thechristfiles.com.au.

Question: What are the advantages of putting on an outreach event at work?

Action: Is it time to put on an outreach event at your workplace? Diarize some time to start planning.

Go with the way God has created relationships

God has made our world to function in particular ways. We live most effectively in God's world when we observe the patterns of creation and live according to them. For example, it's easier to work with gravity than to go against it. So when a friend of mine wanted to get his best time in a half marathon, he chose the flattest marathon course he could. Observing the creational pattern and acting accordingly made his run easier and quicker than it would otherwise have been—the fewer hills the better!

Similarly, God has created human relationships to function in a certain order, and there is wisdom in going with that order rather than ignoring his creational patterns.

The apostle Paul recognizes this as he gives advice to Timothy, a young pastor who was overseeing the Ephesian church:

> Do not rebuke an older man harshly, but exhort him as if he were your father. Treat younger men as brothers, older women as mothers, and younger women as sisters, with absolute purity. (1 Tim 5:1-2, NIV)

Stop and consider: Have ever you thought about applying these principles to sharing Jesus at work?

Older leading younger

God has created the older to lead the younger. So as a general rule it will be easier to talk about Christ at work with someone who is younger. It's more natural for them to show you respect and be willing to listen. Trying to tell an older person how to live is not impossible, but requires a lot of tact.

In the passage above Paul tells Timothy, "Do not rebuke an older man harshly, but exhort him as if he were your father". Timothy is still to rebuke the older man if need be, but he is to do it *gently* and with *respect*. His ministry will be more fruitful if he follows God's creational patterns and treats people accordingly.

As a young accountant, I invited the partner of the firm to an outreach Easter breakfast. I was so nervous as I knocked on the door of his office and invited him along. Surprisingly he said yes and came to the event, but I was so overwhelmed as we walked back to the office that I didn't know what to say as a follow-up.

By contrast, a few years earlier I was able to convince a guy who was about my age to do four *Investigating Christianity* studies with me. Because we were peers, I felt totally comfortable persuading him to read the Bible. In a similar way, when I do 'walk up' evangelism I always try to approach people who are younger than me (I've got more people to choose from these days!). It just feels a lot more natural that way.

I'm not saying that it's impossible to minister to older people. Don't stop trying. But if you have a choice, remember that it's easier to bring the gospel to people who are around your age or younger than you.

Men and women

In the same passage Paul warns Timothy to treat "younger women as sisters, with absolute purity" (v. 2). Paul recognizes the temptations inherent in ministering to people of the opposite sex.

This is good advice for us as we seek to bring the gospel to people in our workplaces. Where you have a choice, it might be wiser to focus on people of the same gender as you. This is because sharing Christ effectively often involves getting to know the other person well, spending time with them and building rapport. Doing this with someone of the opposite gender could easily be misconstrued and it may put you in a tempting situation.

So be wise and careful as you seek to bring Christ to those around you at work. Go with the flow of God's creational patterns and your ministry will be more fruitful and pleasing to God.

Pray: Thank God for his creational patterns and for who he has made you to be. Pray for sensitivity and wisdom as you relate to other people.

Don't let work become too important

God gives us many good gifts to enjoy in this world, and work is one of them. Ecclesiastes recognizes this:

> I perceived that there is nothing better for them than to be joyful and to do good as long as they live; also that everyone should eat and drink and take pleasure in all his toil—this is God's gift to man. (Eccl 3:12-13)

There is enjoyment at work in getting things done, in good friendships, and even in getting an end-of-year bonus for a job well done.

Stop and consider: What do you enjoy about your job?

Potential danger

But sometimes we enjoy our work so much that we are in danger of squeezing out God's priorities for our lives. Over time, a good thing like work can become a godlike thing that takes over everything else.

Here are five potential warning signs that could reveal you love your job just a bit too much:

1. You're not getting enough rest because you are spending so much time at the office.
2. You are afraid to open your mouth about being Christian at work in case you are disadvantaged or ostracized.
3. You find negative feedback at work crushing to your sense of who you are.
4. Your headspace is often dominated by thoughts of work. You can't switch off.
5. You're too busy to care for or develop relationships with your work colleagues.

What to do about it

If you identify with more than one of the statements above, you may be starting to love your work a little too much. "That might be true", you say "but what can I do about it?"

Here are four suggestions:

1. **Work at loving Jesus more.** Somehow you need to take time to meditate again on who Jesus is, his great love for you, and how good heaven is going to be.
2. **Join a work-based Christian group.** Consider joining a Christian group that will encourage you to pray for your colleagues and focus on Jesus at work.

3. **Redraw your boundaries.** My guess is that if you love your work too much, you're probably good at what you do. You are most likely either a valued employee or an owner of a healthy business. This means you'll have collateral to negotiate with as you redraw your work boundaries. Not sure if this will work? You won't know until you try.
4. **Talk to an older mentor.** Find someone who is wise and godly and has your best (Christian) interests at heart. Ask this person if they can meet with you regularly for a while until you get yourself sorted.

It's a great thing to enjoy your work. But remember, heaven is going to be so much better. Make sure you stay focused not just on what is good but on what is *best*:

> "Do not work for food that perishes, but for food that endures to eternal life, which the Son of Man will give you." (John 6:27)

Action: Has your work become too important? What will you do this week to redress your priorities?

Pray: Thank God for your work. Pray that you would have godly priorities in all areas of your life.

Try the direct approach

I became a Christian through a friend of mine boldly inviting me to a meeting where the *Two Ways to Live* gospel presentation was drawn on a whiteboard.[13] My friend followed this up by inviting me to a short course that covered the basics of the gospel message through Bible studies.

Before these invitations, we had spoken very little about Christian things. I liked his direct, no-nonsense approach, and was willing to check things out.

Stop and consider: How did you become a Christian? Was someone bold and direct in inviting or challenging you? Or do you wish people *had* been more direct with you, rather than beating around the bush?

13 *Two Ways to Live* is a simple, clear and challenging outline of the Christian gospel set within the context of the overarching story of the Bible. To view this gospel summary, visit www.twowaystolive.com.

Would we get further?

I wonder sometimes if our strategies to get people to hear the gospel are too complicated and convoluted. Occasionally I hear people say that you need to build a relational bridge with people before they can hear the gospel. But maybe we would get further with more people if we used a more direct approach and just took the gospel straight to them.

An example of what you could say

Here's an example of a more direct and upfront way of bringing the message of Jesus to someone at work:

> "Hey Chris, you know that I'm a Christian—would you ever consider checking out the Christian message yourself?"

Then offer one of these options (or maybe you have a better one):

- "The most famous **verse in the Bible** is John 3:16. Has anyone ever explained it to you?"
- "I could explain the Christian message to you in a few minutes using **drawings**.[14] Have you got a few minutes now, or could we do it over a coffee or lunch sometime?"

14 Each of the six points in the *Two Ways to Live* gospel presentation is accompanied by a drawing to help make the message as clear and memorable as possible. For an explanation of how to draw out the presentation in six squares, see the '*Two Ways to Live* Presentation' video, 6:55, posted by Matthias Media, 28 June 2012 (viewed 5 October 2016): www.youtube.com/watch?v=kbcvuu8lCFg

- “There’s a great **talk online** which sums it up pretty well. It only goes for 20 minutes. Would you be prepared to have a listen when you get a chance?”
- “How about coming to this **event** with me?”
- “This **book** sets it all out pretty clearly, and it’s not a hard read. I’d love to hear what you think about it. Would you be willing to read it?”[15]

Action: Is there someone you could try this direct approach with? How and when will you do it?

15 A great book to give away in this context is *A Fresh Start* by John Chapman (Matthias Media).

Be gracious in conflict

In 2014, Anglican minister David Ould featured in a television program called *Living with the Enemy*, where he spent ten days living with a gay couple. Reflecting on the experience, David commented:

> ...one thing I've learned from the filming, the media work and now people's comments is that a gracious attitude goes a long, long way. The best radio interviews I've had have been those where the interviewer, although opposed to my position, has commented on how much they've appreciated the manner of the discussion.[16]

As David found, one of the most powerful ways to commend the teaching of Jesus Christ to others is to be gracious in conflict.

16 D Ould, 'Living With the Enemy: Some first reflections on the show', *DavidOuld.net*, 4 September 2014 (viewed 6 October 2016): www.davidould.net/living-enemy-lwte-first-reflections-show/

Being gracious is hard

But when we've been attacked or insulted, being gracious is a great challenge. Maybe you've been in conflict with an unreasonably rude person at work. Maybe you belong to a social or sporting club where someone has slandered you behind your back. The natural inclination is to give back as good you get (or even more if possible). I've been involved in some fiery Facebook debates with some very rude atheist friends. I rejoice in the opportunity to interact with them, but find it extremely challenging to stay calm and cool when the insults are flying in my direction.

Stop and consider: Have you ever lost it when you've been provoked or treated badly?

Motivation to be gracious

1. **You're following Jesus' teaching and example.** Jesus commands his followers to love their enemies and to do good to those who hate them (Luke 6:27). Jesus lived out this teaching himself. He was treated with total injustice by his Jewish and Roman opponents. They hated him even though he'd done nothing wrong. Yet Jesus didn't retaliate; instead he entrusted the situation to God (1 Pet 2:23).

2. **You're being a person of blessing.** Followers of Christ are called to be people of blessing, even when insulted, because peace is better than conflict—for both people. And even if the Christian continues to be spoken to harshly, they can rest in the knowledge that God is pleased with their gracious behaviour:

    > Do not repay evil with evil or insult with insult. On the contrary, repay evil with blessing, because to this you were called so that you may inherit a blessing. (1 Peter 3:9, NIV)

3. **You're creating curiosity about the gospel.** Peter expects that when God's people behave graciously under pressure, some people will want to know the reason for their hope:

    > ...but in your hearts honour Christ the Lord as holy, always being prepared to make a defence to anyone who asks you for a reason for the hope that is in you; yet do it with gentleness and respect, having a good conscience, so that, when you are slandered, those who revile your good behaviour in Christ may be put to shame. (1 Pet 3:15-16)

How to respond graciously

Here are some practical tips for keeping your cool and responding to conflict in a gracious way:

- Listen carefully to the person you are in conflict with.

- Reflect back to them what they are trying to say.
- Truly try to empathize with the other person's position.
- Ask yourself: Is this really worth fighting over?
- Pray for strength to be gracious and not to get angry.
- If you feel yourself getting angry, walk away. Go for a walk and re-engage the person once you have calmed down. This applies to email and social media interactions too.

Question: Why should we treat people graciously when in conflict?

Pray: Thank God for being gracious with us, even when we were his enemies.

Rejoice that God uses weakness

Have you noticed the 'funnel effect' in kids' sport? When children are very young they will try anything new. They don't care if they can't dribble the soccer ball with skill and finesse; they are just happy to run around and have a go.

But as the years roll on they become more self-conscious of their abilities (or lack thereof), and drop out of sport because they don't want to look foolish in front of their friends.

Stop and consider: Do you feel a bit self-conscious speaking the Christian message to your work colleagues? Are you so concerned you won't present the gospel in an articulate or impressive way that you end up not saying anything? Are you worried about looking foolish or losing face?

A necessary reminder

The purpose of this rocket is to remind you that God uses weakness to bring about his purposes. I hope this might encourage you to keep trying to speak the gospel message, even when you feel inadequate for the task.

It's helpful to remember that many great heroes of the faith weren't impressive to the naked eye, but God still used them mightily in his plan of salvation. For example:

- **Moses** didn't want to lead God's people, because he was "not eloquent" and was "slow of speech and tongue" (Exod 4:10).
- **Jeremiah** didn't want to be God's spokesman, because "I do not know how to speak, for I am only a youth" (Jer 1:6).
- The apostle **Paul** writes to the Corinthians, "I did not come... with lofty speech or wisdom" (1 Cor 2:1).
- And of course the **Lord Jesus** himself looked weak, powerless and foolish as he was led through the streets of Jerusalem on the way to the cross.

Why does God use weakness?

In 2 Corinthians 4, Paul explains why God often works in this way:

> ...we have this treasure in jars of clay, to show that the surpassing power belongs to God and not to us. (2 Cor 4:7)

The aim is for God to get the glory, not us!

So don't give up speaking the message of the cross

to your work colleagues, even though you may feel inadequate for the task.

Action: Remember this week that God often uses weakness to bring about his eternal purposes. So have a go at talking about Jesus, even when you feel nervous.

Pray: Ask God to give you courage and words to say, even though you don't feel up to the task.

How are you doing with... putting on an outreach event at work? Do you remember the advantages of organizing a work-based event? Are you any closer to arranging one?

Use news and current affairs to talk about Jesus

Stop and consider: Have you ever used a current news story to start a meaningful conversation that points people to Jesus?

News and current affairs can be good tools for turning conversations to Jesus and the gospel in a natural and appropriate way. For example, you could take any headline about the activities of Islamic State (IS) and the awful things done in its name. People at work are likely to have strong opinions on this disturbing subject.

Here's an example conversation (it's based on the story of a planned IS terrorist attack in Brisbane and Sydney that was thwarted at the last minute):

Me: "Hey Mike, what about that terrorist plot that was foiled yesterday. Bit scary, eh?"

Mike: "Yeah, really scary to think that sort of stuff could happen in Australia."

Me: "It's not going to help relations with the Muslim community. Have you noticed how politicians keep trying to separate radical Islam from what they say is *true* Islam—a religion of peace? What do you think?"

Mike: "I think all religions encourage war and violence, and if they come here they should leave their religion at the front door."

Me: "You think all religions lead to war and violence?"

Mike: "Yep, look at the Crusades. The Christians were on the warpath back then. Now it's the Muslims' turn."

Me (plucking up courage): "Mike, I hear what you're saying, and yes—the Crusades don't give Christianity a good name. But violence and retaliation aren't consistent with Jesus' teaching. He allowed himself to be arrested and executed by the Romans; he didn't fight back. And his message was spread by gentle persuasion, not by force. Have you read much about Jesus?"

Mike: "Only at school. But I thought it was pretty boring."

And from there you can move on to talk more about who Jesus really is. I know all conversations don't quite go as perfectly as this one, but it's worth trying.

Principles

Here are some principles of how to turn news and current affairs stories to Jesus and the gospel:

- Try to find a point in the day or week where there's a bit more time to chat. Maybe go out for coffee or lunch.
- Look for tangents to the gospel—for example, conversations about human nature, the purpose of life, evil, hope for the future, relationships, morality and how to motivate people to do the right thing, forgiveness, justice.
- The end aim is not to have an intellectual conversation but to somehow get to Jesus and the gospel.
- Make sure you have listened carefully to the other person's opinions and you understand their position well before giving your opinions. If they feel like you've given them a good hearing, hopefully they will return the courtesy.
- This needs to be done in a natural and appropriate way. Don't force it.
- But at some point in the conversation you're going to need courage to bring up Jesus and Christianity.

▶ **Action:** Look at today's news and pick a story that might lend itself to some interesting conversation and some gospel truth. Try using that story to talk about the gospel.

Make an extra effort to be kind this week

I was lying in bed the other night, just starting to drift off to sleep, when my wife said, “Oh I wish someone would get my lip balm from the bathroom. I’ve got such dry lips.” As there were only two people in the room at the time, I guessed she was hinting that I get up and get it for her. I didn’t move, and selfishly stayed right where I was. I just couldn’t rouse myself to this husbandly act of kindness.

Can you relate to feeling like this at work? Amidst the busyness of your job, do you find it hard to be kind to your colleagues? It’s especially challenging to be kind to those who are difficult to get along with. It’s often easier just to ignore them and focus on your own tasks.

But by being kind to everyone around us—even those we don’t like—we are able to stand out as Christians and witness to the kindness of our God.

Stop and consider: Do you make an effort to be kind to your colleagues?

The power to be kind

How is it possible to be kind given our tendency towards selfish indifference? Well, we need to remember how kind God has been to us in Jesus, even when we didn't deserve it. This is the motivation and power for us to be kind to others, as the following verses remind us:

> Put on then, as God's chosen ones, holy and beloved, compassionate hearts, *kindness*, humility, meekness, and patience... (Col 3:12)

> But when the goodness and *loving kindness* of God our Saviour appeared, he saved us, not because of works done by us in righteousness, but according to his own mercy, by the washing of regeneration and renewal of the Holy Spirit... (Titus 3:4-5)

The Titus 3 passage also reminds us that God has renewed us through the Holy Spirit. The Holy Spirit will help us to bear the fruit of kindness (see also Galatians 5:22).

Be on the lookout

We also need to be on the lookout for opportunities to be kind—for the chance to give an encouraging word, to help someone with their job (even though you are busy), to do a coffee run, to bring in some home cooking, to tidy up after someone without being asked...

We definitely need God's help to go the extra mile in these ways.

Action: This week look out for at least two opportunities to be kind to those around you.

Pray: Thank God that he's been so kind to you in Jesus. Ask him to help you be kind to those around you, at home and at work, even when you don't feel like it.

Remember you are not alone

Sometimes you can feel very alone as a Christian at work.

Do you sometimes wonder, "Where *is* God in this sterile corporate environment?" He is rarely mentioned in conversations; he is seemingly irrelevant to day-to-day life in the office. God felt much closer on Sunday morning, when you were rejoicing with God's people around his word.

Stop and consider: Do you ever question God's presence in your workplace?

Jesus is with you at work

A challenge for each of us is to remember that Jesus *is* with us at work every day—even when it doesn't feel like it.

The Bible reminds us that:

1. **Jesus and God the Father live in us by the Holy Spirit** whether we are at home or at work. As Jesus promises to send the Spirit to his disciples, he tells them:

    > "If anyone loves me, he will keep my word, and my Father will love him, and *we will come to him and make our home with him*." (John 14:23)

2. **Jesus is there with us overseeing our work:**

    > Whatever you do, work heartily, as for the Lord and not for men, knowing that from the Lord you will receive the inheritance as your reward. *You are serving the Lord Christ.* (Col 3:23-24)

3. **Jesus is by our side as we seek to speak to our colleagues about him.** The apostle Paul relied on God's presence as he preached the gospel, even when everyone else had turned their backs:

    > At my first defence no-one came to stand by me, but all deserted me. May it not be charged against them! *But the Lord stood by me and strengthened me,* so that through me the message might be fully proclaimed and all the Gentiles might hear it. (2 Tim 4:16-17)

    And after his resurrection, Jesus told his disciples:

    > "Go therefore and make disciples of all nations, baptizing them in the name of the

> Father and of the Son and of the Holy Spirit, teaching them to observe all that I have commanded you. And behold, *I am with you always, to the end of the age.*" (Matt 28:19-20)

So remember when you turn up at work on Monday morning... you are not alone!

Question: Where does Jesus promise that he is with us always?

Pray: Thank God that Jesus is with you at work today. Pray that you'd be mindful of this as you go about your work and as you seek to share Jesus with others.

How are you doing with... the direct approach? Have you tried the direct approach with anyone yet? How did they respond?

Equip yourself to lead someone to Christ

You are sitting on the train gliding smoothly towards the city centre. You've come in to work a bit later today, so the train isn't quite as crowded. You open your Bible and begin to read. Suddenly the person sitting next to you leans closer and says quietly, "Is that the Bible you're reading?"

You're caught a little by surprise. People don't usually talk on trains. Then it dawns on you that you've seen this person before, walking to and from the station. You've even said "Good morning" a few times as you've passed them by.

Your mind snaps back to the present and you manage to squeak out: "Yes, it is the Bible".

Your neighbour says, "I've always wondered about the Bible. We had a really good Scripture teacher at school and I enjoyed the stories but never really got what it was all about. What's your take on it?"

Your mind begins racing and panic sets in as you do your best to explain what you know about Christianity. You're aware that you are talking a lot, using jargon and putting out lots of complex ideas.

You would love to invite this person to meet again on the train and discuss the Bible more, but you lack the confidence to do this. Out the window the scenery whizzes by... and so does this missed opportunity.

Stop and consider: How would you have fared in this situation?

Invest in training

Are you equipped to make good use of the opportunities God sends your way? Can you share the Christian message in a clear, compelling and succinct way? Are you confident to answer people's objections to Christianity? Are you able to read the Bible one-to-one with an enquirer?

Training is an investment that will not only prepare you for when people ask you about Christianity (like on the train), but will give you more confidence to initiate opportunities. And once you're trained, it'll help you for the rest of your life.

Many of us invest a lot in our careers by doing second degrees or postgraduate study. Is it time for you to invest in being an effective ambassador and mouthpiece for the Lord Jesus Christ?

Training resources

Here are some resources that have helped me to become more confident and able in answering questions and sharing the gospel. Ultimately they've helped me to lead people to Christ.

- ***Two Ways to Live*** is a short gospel presentation you can draw out using six simple illustrations.[17] Memorize it by rote and then practise saying it. The *Two Ways to Live* video-based training course helps you to learn the presentation thoroughly and then shows you how to adapt the basic gospel outline to your own natural patterns of speech.[18]
- ***One-to-One Bible Reading: A simple guide for every Christian*** is a really useful book by David Helm. The guide gives lots of practical advice about reading the Bible with another person, and will equip you to do it with confidence.
- ***So Many Questions*** is a video-based course that will prepare you to answer common questions and objections about Christianity.
- ***Investigating Christianity*** is a set of four Bible studies that get to the heart of the gospel quickly by looking at key Bible passages. The fourth study invites the person to respond and make a commitment in a natural way. Although this isn't primarily

17 For an explanation of how to draw out the presentation in six squares, see the '*Two Ways to Live* Presentation' video, 6:55, posted by Matthias Media, 28 June 2012 (viewed 5 October 2016): www.youtube.com/watch?v=kbcvuu8lCFg

18 For more information, see www.matthiasmedia.com.au/2wtl/trainingcourse.html.

a training resource, doing these studies yourself and knowing these key Bible passages well will increase your confidence in evangelism.

- ***Preparing Just for Starters*** is a self-paced training course that contains everything you need to learn how to use *Just for Starters*, a set of Bible studies that have been used for more than 30 years to follow-up new Christians and establish them in the basics of the faith. By the end of the course you'll have greater confidence in meeting one-to-one to follow-up a new Christian. *Just For Starters* can also be used with 'religious' people who think they're already Christian but are not.

All these resources are published by Matthias Media and are available for purchase at **www.matthiasmedia.com**.

Stop and consider: Which of the above resources would you benefit from most? Where might you find the time and motivation to do some training?

Action: Why not find a Christian friend to be your training partner? Learn together. Practise together. Motivate each other to keep learning in a disciplined way.

Make an effort with the turkeys as well as the eagles

I read some advice in a business magazine that said, "If you want to fly with the eagles then don't scratch with turkeys". It was getting at the idea that if you want to move ahead in the corporate world, you need to hang around the right people—the people who can benefit you—and avoid hanging with the losers.

Your workplace?

Have you noticed people in your workplace who only make an effort with people who can do something for them, but are aloof and lazy in relating to everyone else? Or maybe your boss has his or her favourites. For example, they might only go to lunch with a select few. This kind of behaviour creates division and mistrust in the office, and those who are left out feel undervalued.

Compare this to a CEO I heard of who made the effort to have breakfast each week with small groups of his employees until he had met everyone in the organization, from the most senior person to the least. It can be a great morale booster when a boss makes the effort to treat everyone equally and ensures each person feels valued.

Stop and consider: Do managers and bosses at your workplace have their favourites? How about you?

God's way

In the New Testament, James rebukes Christians who show favouritism. He gives the example of a rich person coming into a meeting and being offered a special chair, then a poor person coming in and having to sit on the ground. James is stinging in his rebuke when he says:

> ...have you not then made distinctions among yourselves and become judges with evil thoughts? (Jas 2:4)

Their thoughts are evil because this is not the way that God treats people. He offers a privileged position in his heavenly kingdom to every kind of person. God does not show favouritism. And we are to love our neighbours whether they are rich or poor—whether they are eagles or turkeys.

So if we were to rewrite that business saying I mentioned from the Bible's perspective, it would go: "If you want to fly with God, make an effort with the turkeys as well as the eagles".

How to love the turkeys

So if you are a follower of Jesus, you need to make an effort to be as considerate to those who are *below* you in the organization as you are to those who are *above* you.

You don't have to stop prioritizing who you spend time with—you still need to get your job done. But as you have opportunity, make an effort to be kind and friendly to anyone who crosses your path, including the cleaners you bump into after hours.

Making an effort to remember the names of subordinates also sends a powerful message that you value everyone equally.

Pray: Give thanks that God's kingdom is for everyone. Pray that you would love everyone equally at work. In your prayers, mention people by name.

Apply yourself to *two* types of work

A number of years ago I worked two part-time jobs. One was for a small furniture manufacturer, the other for the Taxation Institute of Australia. I found it really difficult to juggle two jobs—I felt I was never on top of either one. Although both jobs were in accounting, it always involved a big mental shift going from one to the other.

As Christians at work we face a similar challenge, because God gives us two types of work to do: creation work, and the work of the Lord. We need to keep trying to do both well.

Creation work

Creation work is the work that God gave us in Genesis—to look after the world (Gen 1:28) and to work the garden (Gen 2:15).

After the Fall, work became hard toil and a matter of survival. In Genesis 3, God told Adam, "By the sweat of your face you shall eat bread". In other words, Adam would now need to work the soil in order to feed himself. And, of course, we're in the same boat. Work also became existentially frustrating after the Fall. We work hard only to die and return to the dust (Gen 3:19b).

Renewed motivation to work

In the New Testament our creation work continues, but now with renewed motivation as we work for the Lord (Col 3:23).

Creation work is also an expression of our love for other people: in not being a burden to others (1 Thess 2:9), in caring for our families (1 Tim 5:8) and the poor (Eph 4:28), in supporting paid gospel workers (Gal 6:6), and for the good order of society (Rom 13:6-7).

Jesus is so concerned that you take your creation work seriously that he hints of possible judgement for 'slackers' (Col 3:25) and instructs his apostle to exclude from fellowship those who will not work (2 Thess 3:6).

The work of the Lord

But there's another work that Jesus instructs his people to do. It's "the work of the Lord" and it's found in 1 Corinthians 15:

> Therefore, my beloved brothers, be steadfast, immovable, always *abounding in the work of the Lord,* knowing that in the Lord your labour is not in vain. (1 Cor 15:58)

In the Old Testament this phrase was used to describe the special work in God's temple (see Numbers 8:11 and 1 Chronicles 26:30). Here in this New Testament passage, "the work of the Lord" is the work of *evangelism* and *edification*. I say this because, just a few verses later in 1 Corinthians 16:10, Paul uses this phrase again in relation to the ministry of his offsider Timothy as well as to his own ministry:

> When Timothy comes, see that you put him at ease among you, for he is doing *the work of the Lord,* as I am.

Not in vain

In 1 Corinthians 15:58, the motivation to do "the work of the Lord" is that it's "not in vain". The context of 1 Corinthians 15 is that as people hear the gospel and persevere in it, they will share in the glorious resurrection in the age to come. What a contrast to the existential bleakness of Genesis 3:19! We no longer work only to return to dust; we now look forward to a glorious, eternal future.

Two types of work

So we have two types of work that we are to apply ourselves to: creation work, and the work of the Lord. Some of us might struggle with staying motivated to do our creation work; others might struggle to apply energy to the work of evangelizing the people we work with and edifying the Christians we know. It is a challenge trying to work out the balance between these two types of work, and going from one to the other—but rest assured, Jesus wants us to be working at both.

? **Question:** Why are creation work and the work of the Lord both important?

Action: Which type of work do you think you need to work harder at—creation work or the work of the Lord? How might you go about redressing the balance this week?

How are you doing with... being trained for evangelism? Have you started some kind of training? Have you got a training partner? Do you feel more equipped to lead others to Christ?

Read the Bible one-to-one

There's no greater joy than reading the Bible with a non-Christian who is keen to learn.

I'm reading through the book of Genesis at the moment with a non-Christian man named Sam. Sam is an accountant working in the city. We meet in a food court near his work and are slowly building a friendship. Sam has no biblical background and is fascinated by the stories of Genesis. He has good comprehension skills and asks lots of questions (some of which I can't answer straight away). I'm trying to get Sam to see that Jesus is Abraham's descendant (his 'seed') who fulfills God's promises to bring blessing to the whole world.

Meeting with Sam to read the Bible is one of the highlights of my week.

Stop and consider: What do you think are the advantages of reading the Bible one-to-one?

Here are some that I can think of:

- It's **flexible.** If someone can't make it one week, that's fine. You can just pick up where you left off the following week.
- It's **tailored** to the individual. It's a good environment for your friend to ask questions and to raise objections freely. You can also tailor your answers to best suit your friend's circumstances and background.
- It's **relational.** Meeting one on one is a good way to get to know someone well.

What to read?

Anything in the Bible will do—it's all God's word and it all points to Jesus somehow. That said, starting with one of the four Gospels is probably the best place to begin.[19]

How to run a one-to-one Bible discussion

1. Allow time for a bit of chitchat at the start.
2. Read the passage. Stop at the end of each logical section to discuss it.
3. Ask questions to give some structure. Here are some I use:
    a. What stood out for you? Anything surprising?
    b. Who are the main characters in the story and what do we learn about them?

19 If you're looking for a guide on one-to-one Bible reading, I'd recommend *One-to-One Bible Reading* by David Helm (Matthias Media) or *One-to-One: A Discipleship Handbook* by Sophie de Witt (Authentic Lifestyle).

c. What do we learn about God or Jesus?
d. What questions do you have?
e. What do you think is the main point of the section?
f. If it's true, what are the implications?

4. Say a short prayer at the end if your friend doesn't mind (most people are okay with this). This helps to communicate that it's not just intellectual learning but relationship with God that's on offer.
5. Organize your next meeting.

Leading styles

My preferred leading style is not just to tell my friend the answers (and therefore end up preaching to them) but, where possible, give them time to dig out the answers themselves. This will help them remember what they learn and be more engaged. But some people don't like being put on the spot and may prefer you to point out key truths (this is the approach of *The Word One to One* studies in John's Gospel).[20]

There's nothing more satisfying than reading and discussing God's word with someone who's willing to learn.

20 *The Word One to One* (www.10ofthose.com) is an excellent resource that helps you to walk through John's Gospel with your friends or colleagues. It gives you everything you need for a one-to-one Bible study—the passage, questions, answers and side notes. For more information and free downloads visit the website: www.theword121.com

Action: Can you think of a non-Christian friend or work colleague you could invite to read the Bible with you? How would you go about asking them?

Pray: Ask God to give you the right words and opportunity to invite a friend to read the Bible with you.

Mix and match your Christian and non-Christian friends

At my 50th birthday party I made a special effort to invite a mix of my non-Christian friends (neighbours, relatives, and kids' school contacts) and my Christian friends (mainly from church or work).

There was some intermingling between the groups and I'm sure they asked each other the obvious question, "Where do you know Craig from?" Hopefully this started some good conversations. At the very least, my non-Christian friends got to see that my Christian friends are normal, friendly people.

At the movies

A few years ago, two Christian friends teamed up to go to the movies. They each invited a couple of non-Christian friends to go with them. They chose a movie that might generate some good conversation over dinner afterwards. The night was a great success, thoroughly enjoyed by all.

Two of the women who came that night have since become Christians. I don't know exactly how this night helped these women along their spiritual journeys, but

I'm sure it helped in some way.

Mixing and matching your Christian and non-Christian friends can be a powerful catalyst for the gospel.

Normal and natural

The challenge is to find an event that is normal and natural to invite people to. This is less of an issue for many single people who are keen to meet new people in almost any context. But some of my older friends with families would think it weird that I want them to meet my church friends. So inviting them to a special event like a birthday party or a New Year's Eve party or a Grand Final party, where they might already be expecting to meet a mix of people, would be much more natural.

Action: Use your next birthday to organize a mixed group to go out for lunch or dinner. Diarize it now.

Match

Another tip is to match friends with similar interests. I know a group of Christian guys who go cycling together on Saturday mornings. They've invited other men to the group who aren't Christian. Their interest in cycling binds them together and they have all become good friends. I'm told that good conversations about the 'bigger questions' of life are had while pedaling down the highways and relaxing afterward in the coffee shop.

Action: What interests do you have that you could invite a group of Christian and non-Christian friends to share in?

Pray: Thank God for the good things you enjoy doing with others. Ask God to give you the creativity and energy to mix and match your Christian and non-Christian friends.

Rocket 36

Don't lose heart after a bad experience

John was feeling confident as he met his sister Jacky for lunch that day. He was planning on inviting her to an outreach event at the Town Hall. Jacky had just returned from living in New York for a few years, and had previously shown some interest in Christian things. So John was absolutely shocked when Jacky exploded in anger to John's invitation. She said, "I'm sick of you trying to convert me. Please never talk to me again about Christianity!" John felt depressed and his confidence in the gospel was badly shaken. It took him weeks to recover from this bad experience.

Another work colleague shared that the most discouraging thing for him is when someone agrees to come to an event but then pulls out at the last moment.

And I've heard of many a Christian who's boldly raised an evangelistic topic at work and then got 'smashed' in the argument. They didn't know how to answer people's questions, and they've felt like a fool.

Stop and consider: Have you ever had a bad experience when trying to talk to someone about Christian things? How might you feel if someone responded angrily to your invitation to a gospel event?

Losing heart

Bad experiences can cause us to lose heart and to shrink back from trying to share Christ with people. "I can't do it", you tell yourself. "I'm not an evangelist. It's too risky. I'd better just keep my mouth shut."

Recovery and keeping at it

Here are some suggestions of how to recover from a bad experience and keep going with evangelism:

- **Ask yourself, "Was it really a failure?"** Our job is to give people opportunities to hear the gospel in the most loving, gentle way we can. We can't control how they respond.
- **Learn from your failures.** Ask yourself, "How could I have handled that conversation/invitation better?" Consider whether it's time to seek out some training in handling objections to the gospel.
- **Seek solace and comfort.** Seek solace in God's word and with sympathetic Christian friends. As the apostle Paul says:

> Blessed be the God and Father of our Lord Jesus Christ, the Father of mercies and God of all comfort, who comforts us in all our affliction... (2 Cor 1:3-4a)

- **Change your expectations.** As we noted in Rocket 13, Jesus tells us that few people are on the narrow road that leads to salvation but many are on the broad road that leads to destruction (Matt 7:13-14). We shouldn't be surprised when people reject our invitations or are hostile. And if we are ready for it, it won't be so much of a shock if it happens.
- **Don't lose faith in the power of the gospel to save people.** We should be optimistic. The gospel *does* save people. It saved you. And remember that some people (like the apostle Paul), who were once hostile antagonists, are changed by Jesus and become great ambassadors for him.

Question: How can you recover if you've had a bad experience trying to engage people with the gospel?

Pray: Talk to God about any negative experiences you've had when sharing the gospel. Ask him for perseverance to keep going.

Work at making your Monday morning catch-up more effective

"Hi Harry. How was your weekend?" you ask as you turn on your computer, put your bag down and take the lid off your takeaway coffee.

"Not bad. Went to an awesome party on Saturday night and got pretty smashed. What did you get up to?"

"Oh, watched my son's soccer game and my daughter's netball game, then just lazed around on Sunday."

Boom! Lost opportunity!

Why keep quiet?

Why didn't you mention the two hours you spent at church on Sunday morning? You actually love going to church, so why keep quiet about it? Do you think your non-Christian workmate won't be interested in hearing about church? Well that's partly up to you and how you talk about it!

The 'what did you do on the weekend' conversation on Monday morning can be a great opportunity for you to showcase the benefits and joys of the Christian faith.

Stop and consider: What are your Monday morning conversations like?

Be ready next time

Here are some thoughts about how to prepare something interesting to say for Monday morning:

- **Prepare:** On Sunday, when you are listening to the sermon, take notes, and as the preacher is winding up, **circle one or two key ideas** that might be of interest to your non-Christian work colleagues. Aim to share these truths in a pithy and enthusiastic way on Monday morning.

  For example, last week I heard a sermon on Genesis 38—the story of how the family line of Judah almost died out but was saved by Tamar's initiative when she tricked Judah into sleeping with her. It's a raunchy and fascinating story, suitable for any TV drama. There's a good chance that your non-Christian workmate will be fascinated by a story like this if you do a bit of work to present it properly.
- **Shock:** Part of what we want to do is to **smash the preconceptions** that non-Christians have about church and Christianity. Many people picture church

as an outdated and antiquated institution. Picture the images you get on the TV news on Easter Sunday of men dressed in strange clothes with funny hats, walking down the aisles of medieval buildings. The challenge is to communicate that biblical Christianity can be vibrant, modern and funky.

For example, sharing that you just attended a Christian conference at a modern inner-city venue with 1000 young people might shatter some of those negative images people have.

- **Sell:** Another good thing to do is to communicate that Christianity actually helps you 'do life'. Last Saturday, for example, I went to a men's event at my church. The title of the talk was 'Be a Man of Courage'. I could share in the Monday morning conversation that I was energized to keep trying to be a good husband and father at a time when I'm struggling to do this. Maybe your friend at work is struggling too, and looking for some help.

Action: Next Monday morning on the way to work, prepare your pithy, snazzy line about what you enjoyed about church and how it benefited you. And then deliver it with enthusiasm. It might be the first step to a good conversation or a successful invitation to a gospel event. And try to develop this habit every Monday morning.

Give honest and sincere appreciation

When was the last time someone at work thanked you for a job well done? It's a great feeling isn't it? Your self-esteem tank is filled up and you feel yourself grow an inch taller.

Giving appreciation can be a powerful motivator. So why is it lacking in so many workplaces? Offices are often full of competition between peers who are vying for recognition and success. Managers and executives might withhold positive feedback because they are insecure and feel threatened by bright, talented people who are rising up through the ranks. Maybe people are just so busy trying to achieve unrealistic management targets that they are in 'survival mode' and don't have the headspace to remember to thank other people.

Stop and consider: Why do you think more people at work don't show appreciation to others?

Christians should be different

There are many reasons why Christians should be characterized by giving honest and sincere appreciation:

- **We are freed to love.** Rather than living by malice and envy (Titus 3:3), Christians have been freed to love others. We are secure and strong in our sense of who we are in Christ, and can now look *outward* to the interests of others. After all, we love because God first loved us (1 John 4:19).
- **We value people as created and gifted by God.** We know that every person is uniquely made by God and has unique gifts and abilities. By affirming people we are recognizing God's goodness and power in creation (1 Pet 4:10).
- **Christians are people of gratitude and thankfulness.** Because of God's overwhelming kindness and generosity to us, thankfulness should be at the core of everything we do. And it should overflow into all our relationships (Col 2:7).
- **God commands justice and fairness.** If you are a manager of other people at work, under Christ you are to provide those under you with what is right and fair (Col 4:1). This includes recognizing good work and effort and giving positive feedback where appropriate. People love being appreciated and it will endear you to them as long as your motivations are pure and sincere.

Action: This week make a special effort to be different from the world around you by giving honest and sincere appreciation to the people you work with.

Pray: Stop now and thank God for your work colleagues.

How are you doing with... your Monday morning catch-ups? Have you been prepared to talk about what you learned at church on Sunday?

Make the most of Christmas[21]

The Christmas season is a busy one, but it provides some good opportunities to point people to Jesus.

Here are seven tips that will help you to use the season to explain the reason:

1. **Give Christmas cards.** Buy interesting and thought-provoking Christmas cards to give to work colleagues. Write something affirming in the card and tell the person that you are thankful to God for them.
2. **Give a gospel gift.** Combine a box of chocolates with a Christian book[22] or one of the Gospels with the Christmas story in it (Matthew or Luke).
3. **Ask others about their Christmas traditions.** Use this conversation starter: "What do you normally do on Christmas day?" Then ask (as a natural follow on), "Does Christmas have any religious significance

21 My thanks goes to Tho Luu, who provided some of the ideas for this rocket.

22 For example, *A Fresh Start* by John Chapman (Matthias Media). In recent years there have also been some good Christmas-themed evangelistic books published, such as *A Very Different Christmas* by Rico Tice (The Good Book Company) and *The Curious Sign* by Scott Blackwell (Matthias Media).

for you?" Think about how you would explain the significance of Christmas to a non-Christian.

4. **Email your colleagues a Christmas quiz.**[23] This might stimulate some interest in the 'real' Christmas. There are many myths that people believe are part of the Christmas story that are actually not in the Bible. For example, the Bible does not say that there were three wise men. This implication is drawn from the fact that three gifts were given. You could provide links to the Christmas story in Matthew and Luke so people can read the source documents themselves after their curiosity is aroused.
5. **Invite someone to a Christmas event.** This might be a lunchtime talk, a carols event, or your church's Christmas services.[24]
6. **Organize your own Christmas event at work.** Book a meeting room, organize a speaker, talk title and food, and invite people! Maybe your church pastor might come in to speak for you.[25] Outreach events at work have been done many times before and they work well.
7. **Include others in your Christmas Day lunch.** Some people at work might have families overseas or might come from families that are dysfunctional and/or don't celebrate Christmas. Invite them to

23 For example, 'The Real Christmas Quiz' from *BibleQuizzes.org.uk* (viewed 5 October 2016): www.biblequizzes.org.uk/quiz.php?thereal christmasquiz

24 If you're in Australia, look out for lunchtime events organized by City Bible Forum.

25 Again, if you're in Australia, the staff at City Bible Forum might be able to help you find a speaker.

join you and your family on Christmas Day for lunch.

Action: Which of these ideas can you put into practice? Add them to your 'To Do' list.

Pray: Ask God to give you opportunities for good conversations this Christmas season with workmates, friends and relatives.

Be encouraged—people do become Christians in the workplace!

Lionel's story

My name is Lionel Newcombe. I grew up in England and lost both parents when I was young—my mother when I was three and my father while I was at university.

I didn't have many friends at home, which is why I enjoyed my time at boarding school—I was always in the company of others and could get stuck into sports, in particular my beloved cricket.

When I was in my twenties, my Christian cousin pointed me in the direction of a *Christianity Explored* course in London. But at that point in my life, committing to Jesus felt far too restrictive and boring.

However, after a number of failed relationships and poor work choices, I finally realized I needed Jesus. My boss at the time was a Christian, and despite my less than strong performance at work, he graciously invited me along to a series of Bible talks near our office.

I eventually gave my life to Jesus after another *Christianity Explored* course that was run by the workplace ministry I was connected to. From there I was mentored by a full-time workplace gospel worker, who met with me each week to pray and study the Bible. And a bonus is that we have been great friends ever since.

I've now moved to Australia and am married (to an Aussie) with three young children.

I have the comfort of knowing Jesus as my friend and knowing that he is there for me through whatever challenges life has to offer.

I am also enjoying bringing the message of Jesus to my work colleagues with the encouragement of City Bible Forum.

I still love cricket... have a guess which team I go for?

Susan's story

My name is Susan. I am currently a Senior Consultant at IBM. I am an accountant on paper but an IT consultant in practice.

I come from a non-Christian family and my first encounter with God was through Scripture classes in primary school. I don't remember too much from this other than the free snacks and that I was given a Bible, which I put away into storage for more than a decade.

In 2011, when I was doing my internship at IBM, I met a workmate named Nic. I recall our conversations about God and his faith in Jesus during our one-hour lunch breaks. During this time, he also invited me to his church, but I was hesitant at the time and didn't take up the offer.

It wasn't until mid-2014, when I returned to IBM as a graduate, that I reconnected with Nic. He invited me to a young workers' event put on by City Bible Forum. As Nic was the MC that evening and had generously paid for my ticket, it was hard to say no. The talk I heard that evening really challenged me to think about my priorities in life and it got me thinking about how I wanted to live—so I signed up to do a short course to investigate Christianity. From there I've never looked back.

I am extremely grateful for my new life in Christ. He has blessed me with dear Christian friends like Nic and Caroline. Caroline leads a work-based discipleship group run by City Bible Forum. These people (and others) have been so generous and patient with me—answering my questions, and showing love and concern.

Becoming a Christian has changed me. I have gone from being independent and headstrong, to being vulnerable and dependent on God. More importantly, I know that this life isn't about me; it's about God, my relationship with God, and how I can glorify his name by day and by night. I now spend my Sundays—which were previously empty—serving at church.

I've learned that it's easy to 'talk the talk' but so much harder to 'walk the walk'. As CS Lewis once said, "relying on God has to begin all over again every day as if nothing had yet been done".[26]

I thank God that my workmate Nic kept persevering with me so that I could come to know God through Jesus and have new life.

26 CS Lewis, *Letters of CS Lewis*, rev. edn, Harcourt, New York, 1988, p. 395.

How are you doing with... your workplace evangelism? Which rockets have you implemented since starting this book? Have you been able to talk about Jesus more?

Feedback on this resource

We really appreciate getting feedback about our resources—not just suggestions for how to improve them, but also positive feedback and ways they can be used. We especially love to hear that the resources may have helped someone in their Christian growth.

You can send feedback to us via the 'Feedback' menu in our online store, or write to us at info@matthiasmedia.com.au.

Matthias Media is an evangelical publishing ministry that seeks to persuade all Christians of the truth of God's purposes in Jesus Christ as revealed in the Bible, and equip them with high-quality resources, so that by the work of the Holy Spirit they will:

- abandon their lives to the honour and service of Christ in daily holiness and decision-making
- pray constantly in Christ's name for the fruitfulness and growth of his gospel
- speak the Bible's life-changing word whenever and however they can—in the home, in the world and in the fellowship of his people.

Our resources range from Bible studies and books through to training courses, audio sermons and children's Sunday School material. To find out more, and to access samples and free downloads, visit our website:

www.matthiasmedia.com

How to buy our resources

1. Direct from us over the internet:
   – in the US: www.matthiasmedia.com
   – in Australia: www.matthiasmedia.com.au
2. Direct from us by phone: please visit our website for current phone contact information.
3. Through a range of outlets in various parts of the world. Visit **www.matthiasmedia.com/contact** for details about recommended retailers in your part of the world.
4. Trade enquiries can be addressed to:
   – in the US and Canada: sales@matthiasmedia.com
   – in Australia and the rest of the world: sales@matthiasmedia.com.au

Register at our website for our **free** regular email update to receive information about the latest new resources, **exclusive special offers**, and free articles to help you grow in your Christian life and ministry.

Also from Matthias Media

Gospel Speech

A fresh look at the relationship between every Christian and evangelism

By Lionel Windsor

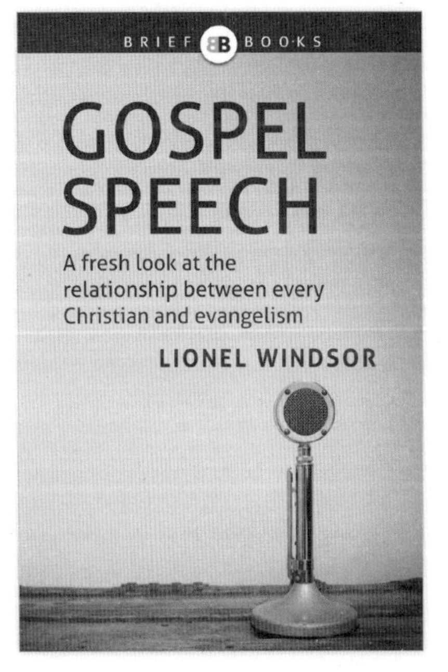

We all have a different relationship with speech. Some of us love it, some of us... not so much. For some it depends a lot on the context: speaking on the phone with a friend is perfectly enjoyable; speaking publicly in front of an audience is our worst nightmare. Some of us speak at a million miles an hour, while some of us have a slow and measured pace, choosing every word carefully. In many ways, speech really is a reflection of who we are as individuals.

But if our speech really is a reflection of who we are, and if being a Christian is a fundamental and even primary way we describe ourselves, should we expect gospel speech to be on our lips?

In this refreshingly different look at what the Bible has to say about evangelism and our speech patterns as Christians, Lionel Windsor shows the connection between faith and speech, and encourages us to confess the Lord Jesus with our lips.

Also from Matthias Media

One-to-One Bible Reading

A simple guide for every Christian

By David Helm

Imagine if there was a way that people could grow in their knowledge of the Lord Jesus Christ—a way that returned gospel growth to the everyday fabric of personal relationship, rather than relying on church-run programs. A way that guided people in a deeper, more meaningful way than an event, program or class could possibly do—on an individual basis by someone who cared for them personally.

What is this way? What is this activity that is so simple and so universal that it meets the discipleship needs of very different people at very different stages of discipleship, even non-Christians?

We call it reading the Bible one-to-one.

But what exactly is reading the Bible one-to-one? Why should we do it? Who is it for?

In *One-to-One Bible Reading: A simple guide for every Christian*, David Helm answers these important questions.

For more information or to order contact:

Matthias Media	**Matthias Media (USA)**
Email: sales@matthiasmedia.com.au	Email: sales@matthiasmedia.com
www.matthiasmedia.com.au	www.matthiasmedia.com